Love
Life

Also by Mario Milosevic

Novels
Claypot Dreamstance
The Coma Monologues
The Doctor and the Clown
Kyle's War
The Last Giant
Splitting
Terrastina and Mazolli

Collections
15 Strange Tales of Crime and Mystery
Entangled Realities (with Kim Antieau)
Labor Days
Miniatures

Poetry
Animal Life
Fantasy Life

Love Life

poems by Mario Milosevic

Green Snake
PUBLISHING

Love Life
by Mario Milosevic

Copyright © 2005 by Mario Milosevic

ISBN-13: 978-1-949644-17-3

No part of this book may be reproduced without written permission of the author.

Published by Green Snake Publishing
www.greensnakepublishing.com

for Kim

Contents

Preliminary Observations

13   Miners

14   Resisting the Patriarchy

16   Someones Loved Me Once

17   Choosing Sides

18   Burglar Alarm

19   Losing It

20   He Had a Really Good First 3 Years

21   When My Mother Comes to Visit

22   One of the Lessons of Life

Field Work

27   Economics

28   Empty Nest

29   The Surface of Lost Time

30   Til Death

31   They Say Everyone Should Have a Will

32   Anniversary

33   Kaleidoscopic Tattoo

34 There's Always the Next Round

35 Soul Mates

36 Strategies and Syllables

37 Tsagaglalal

38 Halve and Have

40 Security

42 Honey Moon

43 The Agreement

44 Life Persists

45 Fairness

46 Human Contact

47 Cold Seducer

48 Thankless Job

49 Old Couple

Practical Application

53 This is the First Place I Touched You

54 Renewal

55 Photo By Me

56 Glow

57 Practicing Conscious Empathy

58 Feeling a Little Seasick

59 Missing You

60 Observing the Leonids With You While You Were Out of Town

61 Soft Visitation

62 Close Up View

63 I've Always Wanted to Heal

64 You Have Seen the Wind

65 Lips Teeth Tongue

66 Always Spring

67 Roses

68 Second Opinion

69 Skamania Landing, 10:30 p.m.

70 Twenty-One Years Later

71 Reunion

72 In Another World

73 Bliss

75 Acknowledgements

76 About the Author

Preliminary Observations

Miners

My father went underground
everyday and clawed

at the guts of the Earth,
sending up chunks of rock

like a rescuer retrieving
body parts after a disaster.

My mother worked hard
finding ways to not think

about what fate
might befall him under

all those tons of ore.
He would sometimes return home

with black smudges on his
cheek or forehead, grimy

kisses of ancient rock.
My mother would reach up

and brush them away
and he'd smile. See,

he would say, I always
come back to you.

Resisting the Patriarchy

It's nineteen seventy.
I'm twelve.
My mother and I take a train
across Canada to visit her
side of the family for the
first time since I was born.
The significance of this fact
escapes me at the time.
Our trip reprises our life
when I was a baby, when
for two years it was just
my mother and me.
Us against the world.

We arrive in Edmonton.
I meet uncles and aunts
and cousins I did not know
existed. I'm too young to
understand their reactions
to me. Too young to see how
some of them pull away,
leave the room, look over
my head. Too young to
understand that they know
I'm the son of an independent
woman who chose her own
way and left her home in the
old country to live her life
on her terms. Too young to
understand, but not too
young to see how,
when they assemble
for a snapshot
on the front yard of

her uncle's house,
her brother tries to
push her to the ground.

Not too young
to see that his awkward
ploy to get her
to be on her knees
is more than a sibling's
prank. Not too young
to see the firm set of
my mother's mouth,
the weariness on her
face, her darkened eyes.
Not too young to see
her refusal to comply
is a larger act. Not too
young to take in the
image of her resistance
and hold it for thirty years.

Someones Loved Me Once

and when they did I did not
know it and could not see

how their love made the shine
of the stars brighter

in a way designed to confound
my own expectations of the

physical laws governing the
glow of bodies burning

in a cold expanse of
gravity's nullifying space

Choosing Sides

My parents: post battle,
mid truce, air toxic
with remembered hurts.
My mother tells us
we will have to move
but our father,
retreated to a hotel room
near his job, will not
be moving with us.

Later in the week
I'm in the school yard,
recess rioting around me,
and see him standing
at the fence searching,
like a soldier scanning
the battlefield for
his missing buddy.

I am camouflaged
by my classmates.
And remain hidden
until he turns from
the fence and I go
back to my classroom
wondering did I
do the right thing.

Burglar Alarm

My widowed mother
who has lived alone
for eleven years
makes jokes at her
hospital job about
how she's so happy
now that her boyfriend
has dumped her.

Outside a car alarm
disturbs the neighborhood
while a blue jay
gets its legs tangled
up in the mesh of
the bird feeder
on our front porch
and some of the nuns
where my mother works

tell her they will pray
for her to find a new
boyfriend. My mother
laughs at the absurdity
of their priorities
and thinks about
how best to offset
the recent down turn
in the stock market.

Losing It

A temper?
I have one.
I've used it
at odd times.
When I was 14
my uncle put
his hand on my
mother's arm
in a casual
gesture that I
saw differently
so I raised
my fist against
him in defense
of her. Ready to
drop him if he
wasn't more
polite to her.
I don't remember
that incident
but my mother
does. She told
me about it
on the phone
today. The time
I set my uncle
straight. A trace
of pride in her
voice that I
liked. A flush
of heat filling
my face like
blood pooling
in a wound.

He Had a Really Good First 3 Years

He said
I was there and
I was the first
person to hold him
after he was born.

He said
we lived in Eugene
and had an organic
garden and he was
well taken care of.

He said
whenever he cried
every single time
one of us picked
him up every time.

He said
he had the best the
happiest childhood
and none of it could
have been any better.

He said
now he won't do things
but he had the best
imprinting years so
he will turn out ok.

When My Mother Comes to Visit

A week before she arrives
I spend my time searching

for places to take her.
Will she like this

museum? Do urban Chinese
gardens interest her?

That waterfall by the
interstate is lovely.

I must find a few simple
restaurants with no

weird food. There has to
be a place where we can

talk for at least a few
minutes. Savoring the

time, each of us recalling,
perhaps, the simple facts.

Before I knew anything
she was my universe.

One of the Lessons of Life

She was still
a child herself,
knocked down by
the birth of her
son. After days
in a hospital bed
unable to move,
she rose and
found her child—
dirty, crying,
hungry—and birthed
an adult's rage.
She called the
furies down to her.
The doctors then
scurrying to do
her bidding. The
rage a good thing.
The red world a
kind of cleansing.

And then, three and
a half decades
later, she's in
another hospital
half a world away
and the doctors
this time say her
husband will die
soon, no hope.
The furies return.
But there is no

making this right.
She grabs the white
coat and flails,
kicks the doctor
in the shins. Does
not stop and the
doctor takes it.
All useless. The
other docs see her
and say this is
good. Depression
is bad but this
anger, this
desperate plunge
after something.
If only this fury
was a universal
passion.

Field Work

Economics

The art of the allocation of resources
seems to ignore the whole issue
of who gets love.
How often and how much.
From who and under
what circumstances.
Have they ever tried
to draw a graph
of love's demand
on the x axis
plotted against love's supply
on the y axis?
It would likely
be too depressing
with x flying off to infinity
and y demarcated
in infinitesimal increments
chronicling the loneliness
of creatures everywhere.

Empty Nest

We put up a bird house.
Watch a pair of swallows
inspect it like a newly wed couple
looking for their first house.

Later we see them mate
on the wing, flutter and frenzy
above the deck railing.

We name them Dash and Lil.
Dash flies off by himself
but always returns. Lil
tends to the home fires.

Two weeks after they move in
a chorus of tiny chirps
fills the birdhouse every time
Dash or Lil enters it.

When we return from the city
one afternoon, we discover
the chirps have disappeared.

We missed all those first flights
and there is no Dash or Lil either.

The bird house hangs empty.
Looking like it needs a FOR SALE sign.

The Surface of Lost Time

His tattoo, stuck on his arm,
watery and blurred
like a house in the distance.

It could have been forty years old.
He had his sleeves rolled up
to the middle of his forearm,

the top of the tattoo
buried under the folds
like the tip of a clock tower

obscured by dark clouds.
Only a woman's name visible
on a once red banner.

I sensed immediately it was not
the name of the woman
standing next to him.

She had her arm around his,
so that her hand,
after some quick maneuvering

covered the name on the banner.
She looked past me.
Somewhere else on the planet

was the woman named on his arm
whom he had expected to love
for year upon year after year.

Til Death

Some couples
(you know
who you are)
achieve longevity
out of spite.

They can be
seen sitting
together and
scowling across
a table, each
one thinking
the same thing:

I'm going to
outlive you,
whatever it
takes. I'm
going to be
the one who
gets the house
the money
the bed
and the remote
all to myself.

They Say Everyone Should Have a Will

She is so sure
she will die first
that he thinks about
making plans
for living alone.

But wait. Now she
revises the scenario
and says: "We will die
together when we
are both very old."

Yes, that is easier.
He can begin making
plans for an after
life where she and
he are eternally bound

with wills that make
legal documents
as irrelevant as listening
to a stranger retelling
last night's dream.

Anniversary

He's in his sixties
and recovering from
a throat cancer that nearly killed
him and made him turn his
life upside down. She's ten
years younger and working in
a career she loves that takes
up most of her time. "I haven't
been lucky in love," she says, "I
haven't found someone I can
be completely in synch with."
It is the eve of our nineteenth
anniversary, and, still naive about
such things, I ask, "But you
do love each other don't you?
You are a couple?" She smiles and
nods. "Yes, but he's in a place in his
life where he wants to play and
he wants a companion to go on
adventures with him but I still
have my painting and my healing
work and I want to spend a lot
of time with that." She shrugs and
smiles again and says, "You are both
lucky." I hold your hand thinking
of our last adventure together. No
one has to tell me I'm lucky. What
I don't understand is why fortune
seems so hard for everyone else.

Kaleidoscopic Tattoo

I will miss this heavy old table
she says to him as they both
maneuver it awkwardly through
the door and down the narrow
stairway to its rendezvous
with the pickup truck that will
take it to the charity sale
making room for their new table
with its polished smooth top and
matching chairs and a day later
he notices the bruise on her shin
where she must have knocked
her leg against the table or the
stair railing as they struggled
sweating and panting with the
barge-like unwieldiness of it and
she runs her finger over the bump
not remembering exactly when
she received this round medallion but
looking forward to the weeks ahead
when the table will return and
linger here under the skin of her leg
making itself known in the
brightening evolving fading colors
of broken blood vessels that fit
right in with what she remembers
of life in the house when that
table was not only good enough
but the best she could imagine.

There's Always the Next Round

You begin by showing a fist: rock.
I counter with a flat hand: paper.
Neither showed the peace sign: scissors.

So I win this round and your scissors
may have to wait for my own mock rock
to smash it to bits like torn paper.

You are perplexed and say on paper
you have figured out that the scissors
should be saved for a time when the rock

cannot rock the paper even with the scissors.

Soul Mates

I think there was a time
when we lived together
before we were born.

We spent our days
painting our version
of the world:

a little green here,
some blue and brown there.
Golden haze
tinting it all

with a deceptive aura
of bracing light,
lifting us
from our pre-life,

pulling us
into the world,
where we
wandered for a time

and found each other,
not remembering
the brush strokes
we applied
before we had hands
or eyes
or heartbeats.

Strategies and Syllables

He's a husband
who seldom refers
to the woman he
stood beside
on his
wedding day
as his wife.

It's a hindrance
of labels
he practices,
attempting to
prevent the
awful whiff
of ownership.

His name
belongs to him.
And hers,
like the color
of the sky,
cannot be
drained away.

He says her
name with
quiet reverence
and feels a
startling inflation
of his spirit
when she says his.

Tsagaglalal

She was a homebound senior
we used to visit regularly,
a molecules thick guardian
anchored to solid rock and
gazing benignly over the cool
quiet river. After some vandals
defaced her sacred visage with
unwelcome markings of their
own, she received far fewer
guests as a way to protect her
from further abuse. We
drive by the road we used to
travel down to see her. I think
of children who grow up and
do what little they can to care
for an aging ailing parent. A
parent who has seen much
more than her children and
carries the weight of time like
an ill fitting burdensome coat,
thinking, how did I end up here
like this?

Halve and Have

You liked the trick for halving
a cake fairly: you cut, I choose.

Remember the half that got away?
You said halving is not the same

as having. We tried it with the
muffin: you skimming off the top.

Was it bigger than the base? Or
smaller? Maybe the same size.

The oddly differing shapes made a
casual decision impossible. When

I chose the piece that looked
larger, you and I consumed the body

and crumbs: evidence of fairness
folded into our bodies. We have

something now, you said. A way of
being in the world that allocates

resources as evenly as possible.
But by this time my eyes had grown

vacant and I know you saw it in me.
We created a world without that

muffin, I said. It seemed a better
world with it. Can we go back now?

Can we choose the half where we
have what we have always wanted?

Security

A paper clip,
clamped silently
over a top corner,

temporarily
binds page to
page, when you

aren't ready for
the commitment
of staples. Later,

if the sheets no
longer seem to
belong together,

you can easily
remove the clip
and send each

separate paper
to its individual
destiny. But if

the mating looks
fully compatible,
you can formalize

the relationship
with a deftly
molded bit of

wire, pushed
through two
puncture holes,

marrying your
slices of processed
tree flesh into

a multi-page
document
that only a

fingernail-risking
maneuver
can dissolve.

Honey Moon

It had seemed like
such a romantic idea
to have the wedding

on the moon but
during the ceremony
the bridesmaids all wore

ghastly blue pressure suits
and the groom's helmet
tilted oddly away

from the bride
who suddenly felt
light-headed in one-sixth gee

but nevertheless endured
a profound sinking heart
seeing her husband-to-be's face

eyes wide behind his visor
and his gaze roaming longingly
over the smooth cool powder

of Luna's silver-gray flesh
her exquisite inviting skin
like dry gasps of wonder.

The Agreement

This storm will pass, he thought. You
will want to hear from me. You will

want to know. She thought, that water,
it talks. Whose voice from the other

side? If I go first, he said, I'll send
you a message, ok? Will you wait for it?

He wanted to make this deal with her.
She said why? If you're gone

a message won't help me. Or you.
But then, he said, you'll know,

that there is something after this.
She said, my father is there. He hasn't

sent a message. She said, if there is no
message, what does that mean? He could

not speak. Only saw the rain drops
slithering down the window pane, leaving

tracks of hydroglyphics, wet shapes like
rock paintings done by anonymous ancestors.

Life Persists

In one form or another
it seems life is always there:

sculpting the energy of the planet
into these oddly unstable

accumulations
of flesh and process:

executing a plan laid down
eons ago but deviating

from the script
long enough

to make you wonder:
Why can we stop

and consider the mechanisms
that brought us to this place

when the knowledge
won't bring us food

or save us
from being food

or draw us closer
to a possible love?

Fairness

A couple we know
split up after 14 years.
The one who got dumped
bought an old camper
and went on the road
with the dog.
Old dog with maybe
a dozen dog years left in her.
Only fair for the hurt one
to keep the pet.
And I'm sure the dog was ready
to comfort her
on her sad journey
but what of the dog?
Wouldn't she have benefited
from being with the other half,
the one who was enjoying
the best year of her life?

Human Contact

I ask someone who was there,
what was it like living through
World War II. I imagine she will answer
with stories of hardships,
rationing and fear,
grief for fallen sons and brothers,
uneasy feelings that her civilization
was about to dissolve.

It brought us closer together
she says. Neighbors helping neighbors.
We brought food to each other
and spent evenings together just talking.

Behind me the television, tuned
to the latest conflict, green explosions
flowering the screen, draws her gaze
away from me. She has listened
to my questions long enough
and goes to sit beside her husband.
Holding hands, they watch the war.

Cold Seducer

She scrambles your senses.
Uses any ploy to get you into bed.
Makes you sweat and strain,
clogs you up with her embrace.

The thing is she knows you so well.
Has fitted herself to your body
so many times before.
Understands your weak points.

The tender spot at your throat
is where she usually begins.
Later she'll make your head spin
and stuff your sinuses.

It's all designed to crush
your defenses and welcome her
into your being. She'll be
devoted to you for a week.

Sleep with you every night.
But then you will bore her.
She will pick up and move on
while you ask why me why now.

Thankless Job

It's easy to tell
when someone's been a parent
for too long.
You ask her what she's doing
these days
and she tells you
about her son's new job
or her daughter's choice of graduate school
or how she wishes
she could see her grandchildren
more often.

Old Couple

She shelters him
like he's still the boy
he was before
they ever met. He
says nothing, as
always, saving
words for those
times when he
wants to make
her laugh or show
her he's still the
man she has loved
intermittently
for six decades.
She remembers
him before the
wrinkles, before
the slow gait,
before his
acquiescence to
the forces that
over-ripened
his body and
buried his essence
before his time,
before her time.
He'd like to go
home, build a
tree house in the
back yard, invite
her in. Talk about
the future before
it's the past.

Practical Application

This is the First Place I Touched You

This is the first place I touched you.
It was a wilting East Lansing summer
and this is the first place I touched you.
You wore that bare-backed dress
and this is the first place I touched you.
I was uncharacteristically bold and
this is the first place I touched you.
As I recall it now, the middle vertebra
was the first place I touched you.
You didn't move away when I put my hand
on the first place I touched you.
And even now I place my palm
on the first place I touched you
and it brings back that Michigan August
and the first place I touched you.

Renewal

Here is the spirit of love
the way mates live their lives:

That even when we have been apart
memory insists we were together.

Footsteps a harmonious fugue,
sides bumping, hands entwined,

essences embracing and embraced.
Conjuring a necessary solidity

out of the thinnest of vapors.
And seeing, yes, remembering the

past as a kind of rehearsal for
a shared and sustaining future.

Photo By Me

But I only tripped
the shutter.
You painted the
image, your skin
a long distance
brush loaded with
clumps of photons.
How you maneuvered
the paths of them
through the lens
to splash onto
the glossy rectangle.
It looked effortless,
a practiced skill
that must seem like
second nature now.
And all in the space
of a split second.
First touch
best touch.
Don't think on it
too long. Take the
credit for yourself.
I'll release my
hold on the picture.
I'll let it go for you.

Glow

Remember that year in Tucson.
You laboring at U of A for a
Master's degree, having given
up the dream of being a writer.
Me banging a keyboard at a Mom
and Pop type shop that went
out of business, shocking us both
with the thought of what do we
do now. Remember how we used
to drive up the foothills of the
Catalina Mountains north of
town in the warm evenings.
We'd park at the side of the road
and get out and lean against the
car and watch the lightning flashes
over the city. A dozen years later
we still have that car with the dent
from where one of us put too much
weight on the flimsy hood. Tucson
was noisy, stifling, and hot, blighted
with ugly sprawl, but it was magical
under those sky fissures, momentarily
lit up like a vision in the desert.
Those brief illuminations a fleeting
electric opportunity for clear-eyed
contemplation and a reminder of
how nothing else really mattered
when we were close enough to
hold hands and feel the heat of
each other on our skins.

Practicing Conscious Empathy

The grasshopper
burning in the sun
dries your skin

and the woman
with the small baby
tires your bones

and the house guest
with the hurt heart
silences your voice

and the sister with
the cold sore
corrupts your lip

and the world
with its opulent
intricate web

rebirths you
with the miracle
of a healing life.

Feeling a Little Seasick

Here's where it gets kind of scary.
She tells me she has expectations.
They are culturally imposed, certainly,
but nevertheless they are there:
how she likes me to be the steady one
not freaking out at things like she
sometimes does, and like I never
used to.   This sobering bit of news
comes after my kidney stone episodes
which have turned me into a ginger soul
stepping lightly as a ghost might,
unsure of just how substantial
my claim to the world is.
                    My steadiness,
so long a given, has now become a
question about where did the old
reliable things go, like cars that you
could work on or service that made
you feel special.
              And I monitor my
body for signs that some new crisis
will arrive in the night, maybe, or the
early morning, before I'm up and solid
and able to bail water if necessary
or bring the boat to harbor, all the while
making it look easy.

Missing You

Your dirty socks on the bedroom floor
remain like cushiony footprints
in the spot where you left them.
I don't put them in the basket
as I tidy up a bit. Your partially
eaten apple, teeth marks raking the
flesh, looks like a bronzed sculpture
resting on the pedestal of the end table.
No way I'm going to put it in the trash.
It's a quiet night. Then the motor of the VCR
whines into life to record an episode of
ER you didn't want to miss. I listen
to the tape unwinding its hiss into the
room, drinking up images of a stormy night
at the make believe hospital and remember
you don't like doctor stories or shows
where people suffer or have diseases.
The apple keeps turning browner. The edges
of the skin have dried up and curled toward
the heart and I remember, the way I recall
the feel of your cheek against my hand, that
a squirt of lemon juice would have
gone a long way to preserving that fruit.

Observing the Leonids
With You While You
Were Out of Town

Weren't you there?
Not beside me, but
there under the same

stars, tears burning white
trails across the face
of the sky? It was you

I thought of when I pointed
up and exclaimed at the
brightness searing my

retina. And yours too?
Awake at two ayem,
was it our bond that

lit up the night? My wish
on a falling star that
you would soon be home?

Soft Visitation

Night angel,
dream maker.

You arrive,
sing silent songs
of Earth.
We embrace
the shadow warmth
around us.

Quiet wings,
dream maker.

Close Up View

The strands of your hair
like interstate highways,
the routes of them
sliding against each other
in a spaghettied order
of elaborate exits.

There are no signs,
and it's all been made
by a brush,
held in your hand,
infused with magic.

A million road trips
there in the map
atop your head.
Untangled and smoothed out.
A million ways in.

I've Always Wanted to Heal

I've always wanted to heal
you say
when we talk of the things
that move our souls.

I think of you
dismantling a broken clock
into its tiny parts
and reconstructing its workings
so it tells the correct time again.

You probably don't think of this
as a healing
but no laying on of hands
could create a more miraculous cure.

You Have Seen the Wind

You have seen the wind
and tasted the moon.
You know the sound
of flowers singing,
and inhale the aroma from
the stones of the Earth.
The world holds you.
Eternal time caresses
and warms you
to celebrate the days
of your birth.

Lips Teeth Tongue

Only after your bath
will you allow me the
pleasure of kissing the
soles of your feet and

the wrinkles of your toes.
My voice is muted here
where the apparatus
of my speech meets the print

you apply to the Earth.
I do not think of words
except the quiet ones
made from the syllables

of your silence that seems
to say: keep talking
I like that last sentence
and I'd love to hear more.

Always Spring

The twisting of the vine
  insures a tangled life;
and our close-knit design
  protects our ties from strife.

Now see the flowers grow
  along the turning strand—
each season we will know
  our union's fresh dreamland.

Roses

Earlier today
I came into the house and saw
seven roses in a vase
on the kitchen table.

Their petals were spread wide,
swollen from the water you poured
saturating their stem ends.

I thought of you
bringing roses home from town
for me.

You let their molecules
flood the house with flower smells
that I gladly swam through
to find your comforting touch.

Second Opinion

Will you feel my breasts? she asks
in a voice touched by fear,
for this is no erotic invitation
but a sober request for exploration.

Men in glaring clean little rooms,
wearing white lab coats and serious tones,
have explained how she can examine
her breasts for errant growths.

So she has evolved a monthly ritual
carefully insuring that all
is well. And when she is done
she needs confirmation of her findings.

Her husband carefully follows the
prescribed method, until a minute
or so later he declares
everything is A-OK and she,

heart rattled by adrenaline,
tries to tuck the fear away.
And wonders why she has to think
about her own cells betraying her.

Skamania Landing, 10:30 p.m.

We sit on the bloodstained
bench at the end of the dock
where some of the Columbia's
fish have endured their last few
minutes.
        We watch the moon's
reflection dappling the black
water.
     Periodic splashes in the
darkness testify that not all of the
river's citizens have succumbed
to fishing rod and club.
          We say:
wouldn't it be fun to bring out
a sleeping bag and spend the
night here.
       Here on this strand
of the ocean that has rolled into
the gorge and rises now toward
the moon hanging above us,
the moon bathing you in
unexpected light.
        The moon
spread out on the water like
a path of silver stones leading
to an awakening on the unseen
distant shore.

Twenty-One Years Later

After you came back from lunch
with your old boyfriend
I didn't want to hear about his life.
We said goodbye you said.

Is it for real this goodbye?
I had visions of him e-mailing you,
a renewed friendship developing,
his life creeping into our life.

My hand felt big on the end
of my arm like a useless weight.
Outside the window the red and yellow
leaves on the oak and maple trees
shivered. The rain drops seemed to
brighten the colors and the gray
of the quiet sky made me think of
dead wood after it has been
blown smooth by sand and wind.

Reunion

Maybe it's hard to believe
these rocks and this river
were there at your birth
and have watched over your life.

You stand sky clad,
the air laden
with white water mist,
your arms raised
like tree branches,
toes rooting you
to your infant
guardians wondering
where have you been
all these years.

In Another World

On the radio
they're talking about
discovering planets
orbiting other stars.
I listen closely
while you look
far away.
I'll put together
an expedition
to retrieve you
from one of those
extra solar worlds.
There's a home
waiting for you here.

Bliss

You turn up
Annie Lennox
dance with air
pull me up
away from
my book
we twirl
jump
sweat
embrace
laugh
until Annie
falls silent
and the house
is just us
holding hands
and warming
the air
with our
breath.

Acknowledgements

The poems in *Love Life* are previously unpublished, except as noted here:

"Choosing Sides" originally appeared in *Nerve Cowboy* #14, Fall 2002.

"Honey Moon" originally appeared in *Asimov's SF*, March 2005.

"In Another World" originally appeared in *Star*Line*, #25.6, November/December 2002.

"I've Always Wanted to Heal" originally appeared in *Free Verse*, January 2004.

"Resisting the Patriarchy" originally appeared in *Möbius*, vol. 17, #2, Fall & Winter 2002.

"Security" originally appeared in *Into the Teeth of the Wind*, vol. II, Issues 2-3, 2001.

"Twenty-One Years Later" originally appeared in *Into the Teeth of the Wind*, vol. IV, Issues 2-4, 2004.

About the Author

Mario Milosevic spent his first year of life in a refugee camp in Italy. His poems have appeared in many print and online journals and anthologies. His two previous collections of poetry, *Animal Life* and *Fantasy Life*, were published in 2004. He lives with his wife, writer Kim Antieau, near Mt. St. Helens, where they await the next big eruption.

www.ingramcontent.com/pod-product-compliance
Lightning Source LLC
Chambersburg PA
CBHW020121130526
44591CB00031B/245